STEPHEN BIESTY

ROME

In Spectacular Cross-Section

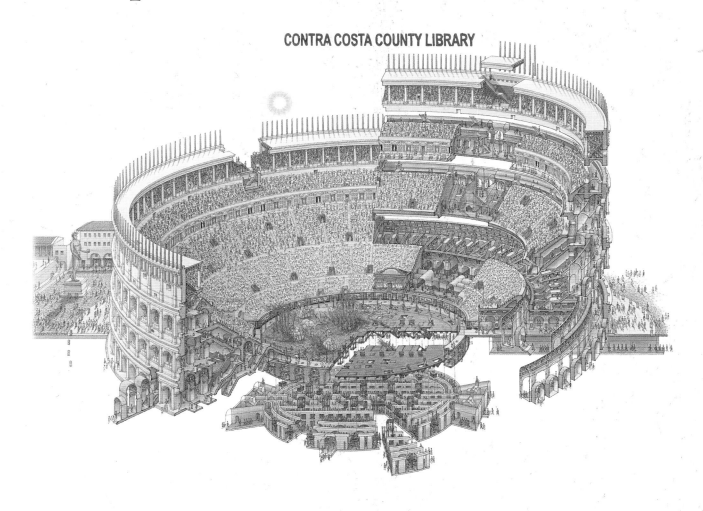

Text by Andrew Solway

Consultant: James Morwood (Wadham College, Oxford)

Oxford University Press
Great Clarendon Street, Oxford, England OX2 6DP

Oxford is a registered trademark of Oxford University Press in the UK and in certain
other countries.

Library of Congress Cataloging-in-Publication Data
Solway, Andrew.
Rome: in spectacular cross-section / written by Andrew Solway; illustrations by
Stephen Biesty.
p. cm.
Includes index.
Summary: Detailed illustrations with explanatory captions and narrative text survey
some sites in ancient Rome, including the house of a wealthy family, the Colosseum,
the Baths of Trajan, and the Temple of Jupiter.

1. Rome—Social life and customs—Juvenile literature. 2. Rome—Civilization—Juvenile
literature. [1. Rome—Social life and customs. 2. Rome—Civilization.] I. Biesty, Stephen,
ill. II. Title.

DG78 .S68 2003
937—dc21   2002070694

0-439-45546-4

10 9 8 7 6 5 4 3 2 1   03 04 05 06 07

Printed in Italy
First printing, April 2003

A Note on B.C./A.D. Abbreviations

Throughout this book, you will see that dates appear with the abbreviations "A.D." and "B.C." These terms are used to keep track of years in the Gregorian calendar, which is the one commonly used today. In the Gregorian calendar, years are counted from the year in which Jesus Christ was thought to have been born. Any year after this is written with the letters A.D. before it (for example, A.D. 2003). "A.D." stands for the Latin words "Anno Domini," which mean "in the year of the Lord." Years before the birth of Jesus Christ are counted backward and have the letters B.C. after them (for example, 55 B.C.). "B.C." stands for "before Christ." Sometimes people choose to use the abbreviations B.C.E. (meaning "Before the Common Era" or "Before the Christian Era") and C.E. (meaning "Common Era" or "Christian Era") instead of B.C. and A.D.

Contents

Titus Cotta and Marcus Cotta Maximus

Titus Cotta is the son of an important Roman senator named Marcus Cotta Maximus. They live in an elegant house on Viminal Hill, not far from the center of Rome. Titus doesn't go to school; he has lessons with his own tutor. But today is a festival day, so there are no lessons. Titus and his father have a busy day planned.

Rome, A.D. 128

This is the city of Rome in the year A.D. 128. It's the biggest city in the ancient world — more than a million people live here. And it's at the center of a huge empire stretching all the way from Egypt to Britain.

Today is the festival of the twin gods Castor and Pollux. There's a parade this morning, so people are making an early start. One of them is Titus Cotta Maximus. His father, Marcus, has promised to take him to the Colosseum and to the chariot races.

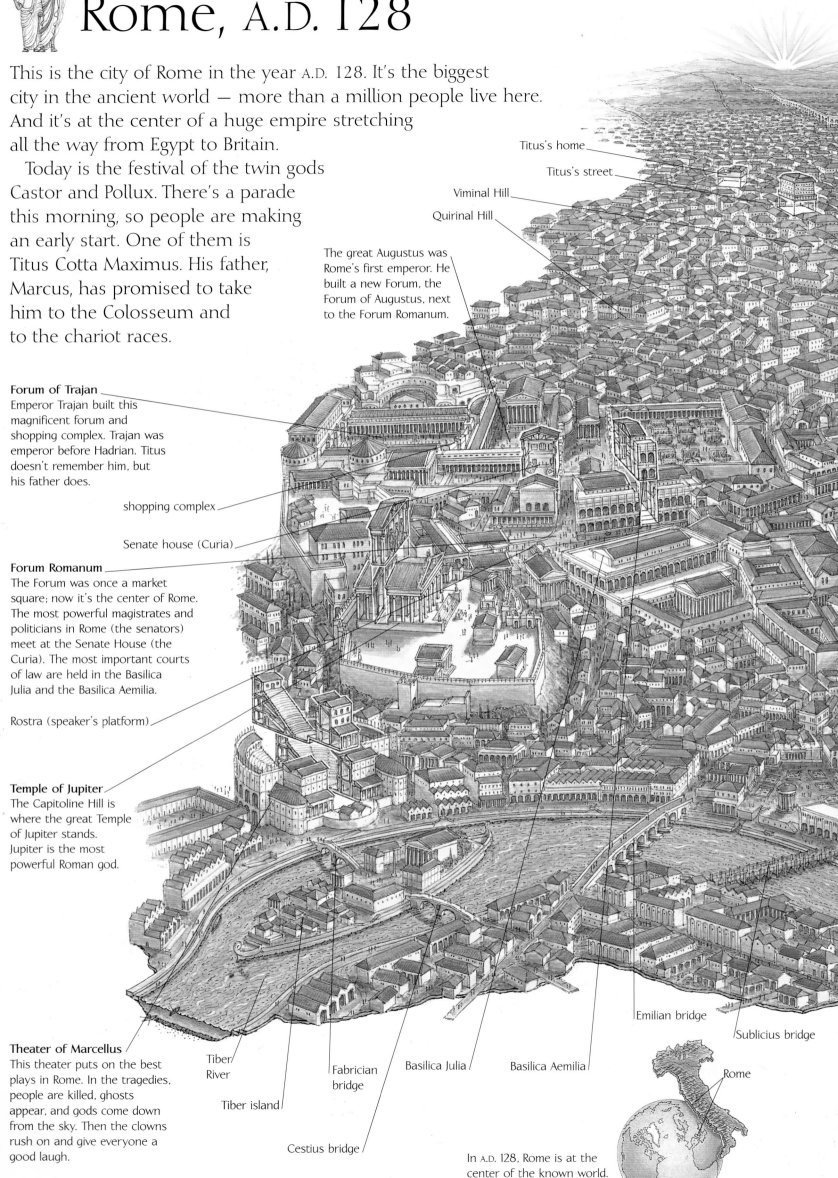

Titus's home

Titus's street

Viminal Hill

Quirinal Hill

The great Augustus was Rome's first emperor. He built a new Forum, the Forum of Augustus, next to the Forum Romanum.

Forum of Trajan
Emperor Trajan built this magnificent forum and shopping complex. Trajan was emperor before Hadrian. Titus doesn't remember him, but his father does.

shopping complex

Senate house (Curia)

Forum Romanum
The Forum was once a market square; now it's the center of Rome. The most powerful magistrates and politicians in Rome (the senators) meet at the Senate House (the Curia). The most important courts of law are held in the Basilica Julia and the Basilica Aemilia.

Rostra (speaker's platform)

Temple of Jupiter
The Capitoline Hill is where the great Temple of Jupiter stands. Jupiter is the most powerful Roman god.

Emilian bridge

Sublicius bridge

Theater of Marcellus
This theater puts on the best plays in Rome. In the tragedies, people are killed, ghosts appear, and gods come down from the sky. Then the clowns rush on and give everyone a good laugh.

Tiber River

Fabrician bridge

Basilica Julia

Basilica Aemilia

Rome

Tiber island

Cestius bridge

In A.D. 128, Rome is at the center of the known world.

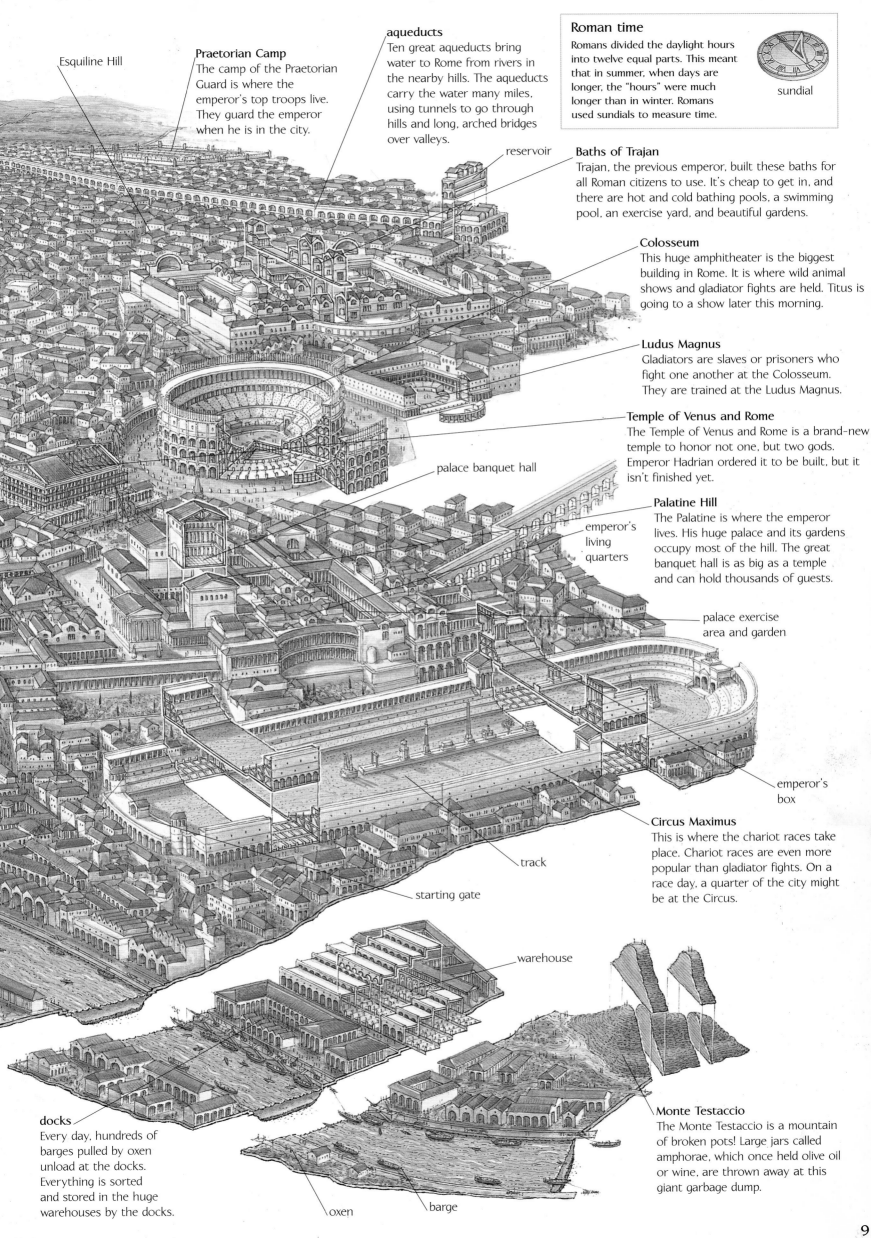

Esquiline Hill

Praetorian Camp
The camp of the Praetorian Guard is where the emperor's top troops live. They guard the emperor when he is in the city.

aqueducts
Ten great aqueducts bring water to Rome from rivers in the nearby hills. The aqueducts carry the water many miles, using tunnels to go through hills and long, arched bridges over valleys.

reservoir

Baths of Trajan
Trajan, the previous emperor, built these baths for all Roman citizens to use. It's cheap to get in, and there are hot and cold bathing pools, a swimming pool, an exercise yard, and beautiful gardens.

Colosseum
This huge amphitheater is the biggest building in Rome. It is where wild animal shows and gladiator fights are held. Titus is going to a show later this morning.

Ludus Magnus
Gladiators are slaves or prisoners who fight one another at the Colosseum. They are trained at the Ludus Magnus.

Temple of Venus and Rome
The Temple of Venus and Rome is a brand-new temple to honor not one, but two gods. Emperor Hadrian ordered it to be built, but it isn't finished yet.

palace banquet hall

Palatine Hill
The Palatine is where the emperor lives. His huge palace and its gardens occupy most of the hill. The great banquet hall is as big as a temple and can hold thousands of guests.

emperor's living quarters

palace exercise area and garden

emperor's box

Circus Maximus
This is where the chariot races take place. Chariot races are even more popular than gladiator fights. On a race day, a quarter of the city might be at the Circus.

track

starting gate

warehouse

docks
Every day, hundreds of barges pulled by oxen unload at the docks. Everything is sorted and stored in the huge warehouses by the docks.

oxen

barge

Monte Testaccio
The Monte Testaccio is a mountain of broken pots! Large jars called amphorae, which once held olive oil or wine, are thrown away at this giant garbage dump.

Titus's house

It's only just light, but at Titus's house everyone is busy. Because today is a festival day, Titus and his father will be out for the whole day, going to the Temple of Jupiter and visiting the games and the races. Titus's mother and baby sister stay at home. In the evening, the family is going to host a festival-day feast to celebrate.

rainwater spouts

atrium
The first room you come into is the atrium. This is a large hallway with a small pool in the center. There are stone carvings of Titus's ancestors around the atrium.

carvings (busts) of ancestors

doorway
At night, the front door is guarded by a doorkeeper— a household slave with a guard dog. Titus and his family are rich, so they have many slaves. Slaves can be bought and sold at slave markets. They do most of the work around the house.

clients

water supply
Titus's family is lucky — they have a well in the house. Not many Roman houses have their own water supply.

bronzesmith's shop

shops
The two rooms that face the street are rented out as shops. The owners sleep above the shop at night. This morning they are already hard at work.

pool (*impluvium*)

street

mosaic floor

slave

pet cat

Titus
Titus isn't dressed yet. The cook gave Titus some bread for breakfast. He gives a piece to his cat.

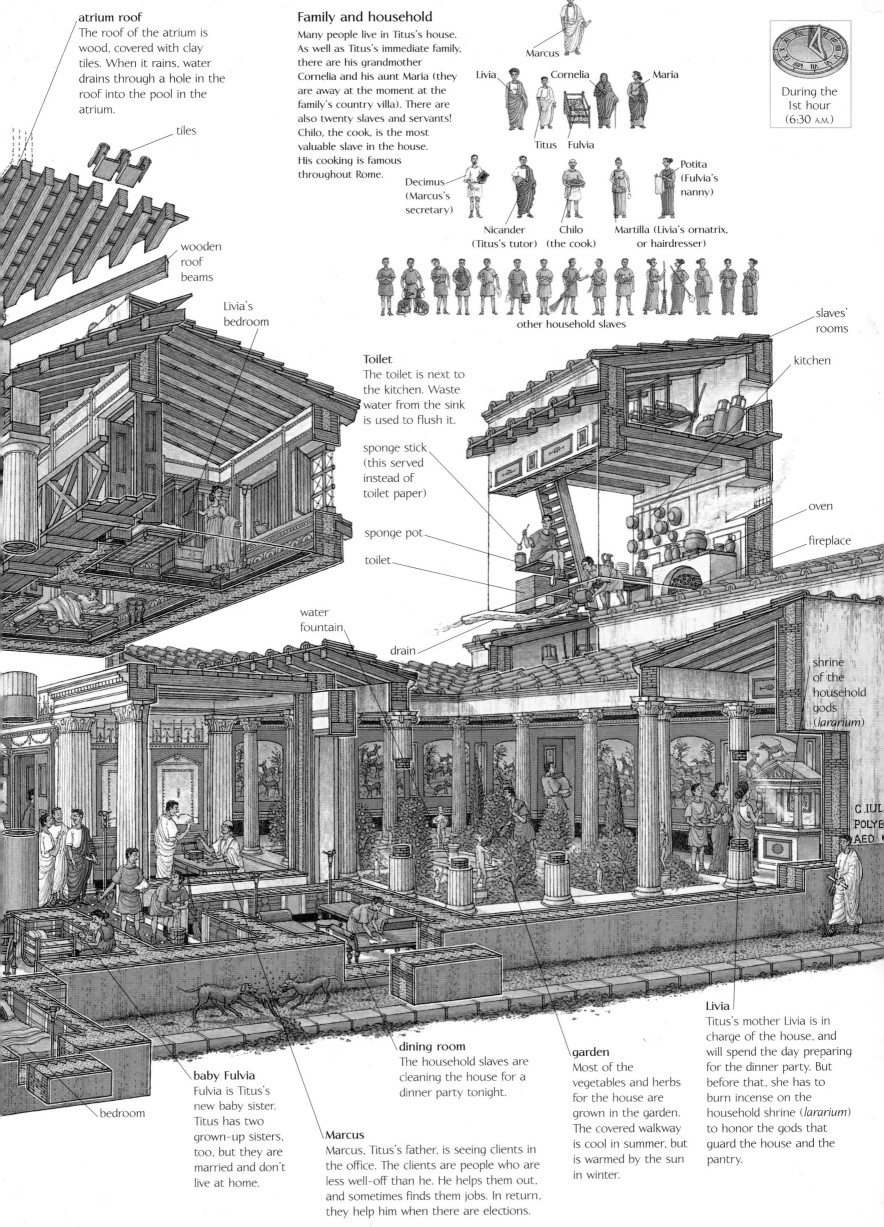

atrium roof
The roof of the atrium is wood, covered with clay tiles. When it rains, water drains through a hole in the roof into the pool in the atrium.

tiles

wooden roof beams

Livia's bedroom

Family and household
Many people live in Titus's house. As well as Titus's immediate family, there are his grandmother Cornelia and his aunt Maria (they are away at the moment at the family's country villa). There are also twenty slaves and servants! Chilo, the cook, is the most valuable slave in the house. His cooking is famous throughout Rome.

Marcus

Livia   Cornelia   Maria

Titus   Fulvia

Decimus (Marcus's secretary)

Potita (Fulvia's nanny)

Nicander (Titus's tutor)

Chilo (the cook)

Martilla (Livia's ornatrix, or hairdresser)

other household slaves

During the 1st hour (6:30 A.M.)

Toilet
The toilet is next to the kitchen. Waste water from the sink is used to flush it.

sponge stick (this served instead of toilet paper)

sponge pot

toilet

water fountain

drain

slaves' rooms

kitchen

oven

fireplace

shrine of the household gods (*lararium*)

C. IUL POLYE AED

baby Fulvia
Fulvia is Titus's new baby sister. Titus has two grown-up sisters, too, but they are married and don't live at home.

bedroom

Marcus
Marcus, Titus's father, is seeing clients in the office. The clients are people who are less well-off than he. He helps them out, and sometimes finds them jobs. In return, they help him when there are elections.

dining room
The household slaves are cleaning the house for a dinner party tonight.

garden
Most of the vegetables and herbs for the house are grown in the garden. The covered walkway is cool in summer, but is warmed by the sun in winter.

Livia
Titus's mother Livia is in charge of the house, and will spend the day preparing for the dinner party. But before that, she has to burn incense on the household shrine (*lararium*) to honor the gods that guard the house and the pantry.

In the street

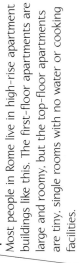

Titus and his father set off for the Temple of Jupiter. On the way, they stop at the bakery near their home to talk to Hermes, the owner. Titus munches on a pizza while his father and Hermes talk business. Hermes is a freedman, or freed slave. He used to be the cook at Titus's house, but then he bought his freedom from Titus's father.

apartments
Most people in Rome live in high-rise apartment buildings like this. The first-floor apartments are large and roomy, but the top-floor apartments are tiny, single rooms with no water or cooking facilities.

top-floor rooms

concrete

bricks

apartment walls
The walls of the apartment are made of concrete, covered with pyramid-shaped bricks pressed point-first into the wet concrete. The bricks are then covered with plaster.

first-floor apartment

portico
Fires are always breaking out in Rome. The emperor Augustus ruled that buildings had to have a walkway (portico) above street level to help firefighters get at fires.

aqueduct bringing water from the hills

carts
Carts are banned from the narrow streets during the day, unless they are carrying building supplies. This one is bringing wood for a damaged building.

Titus's home

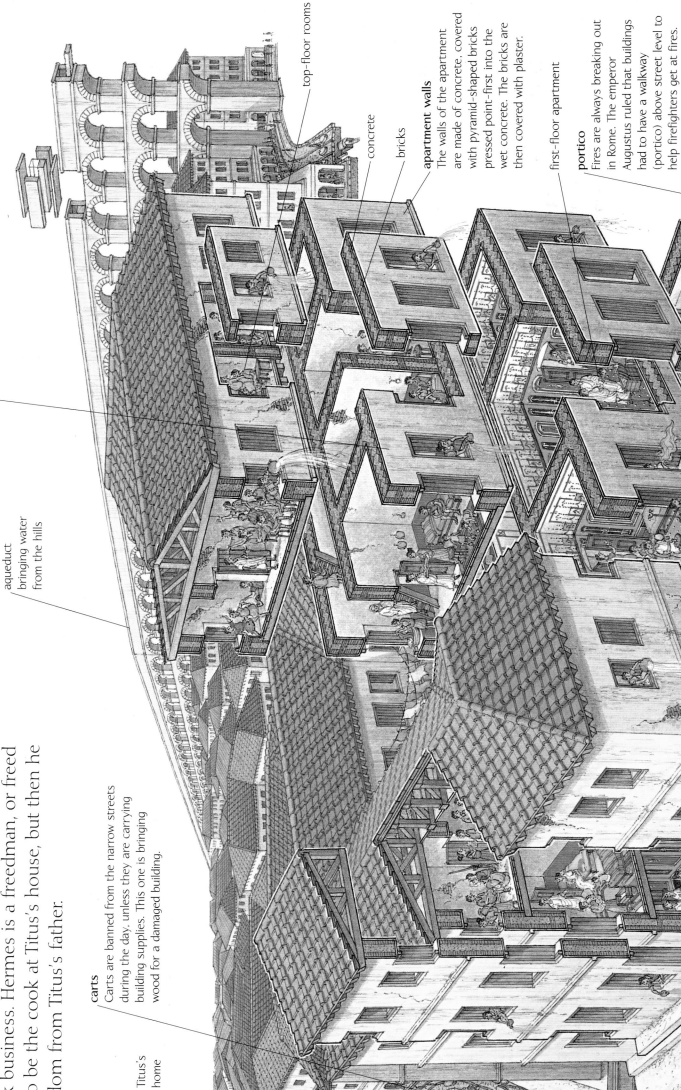

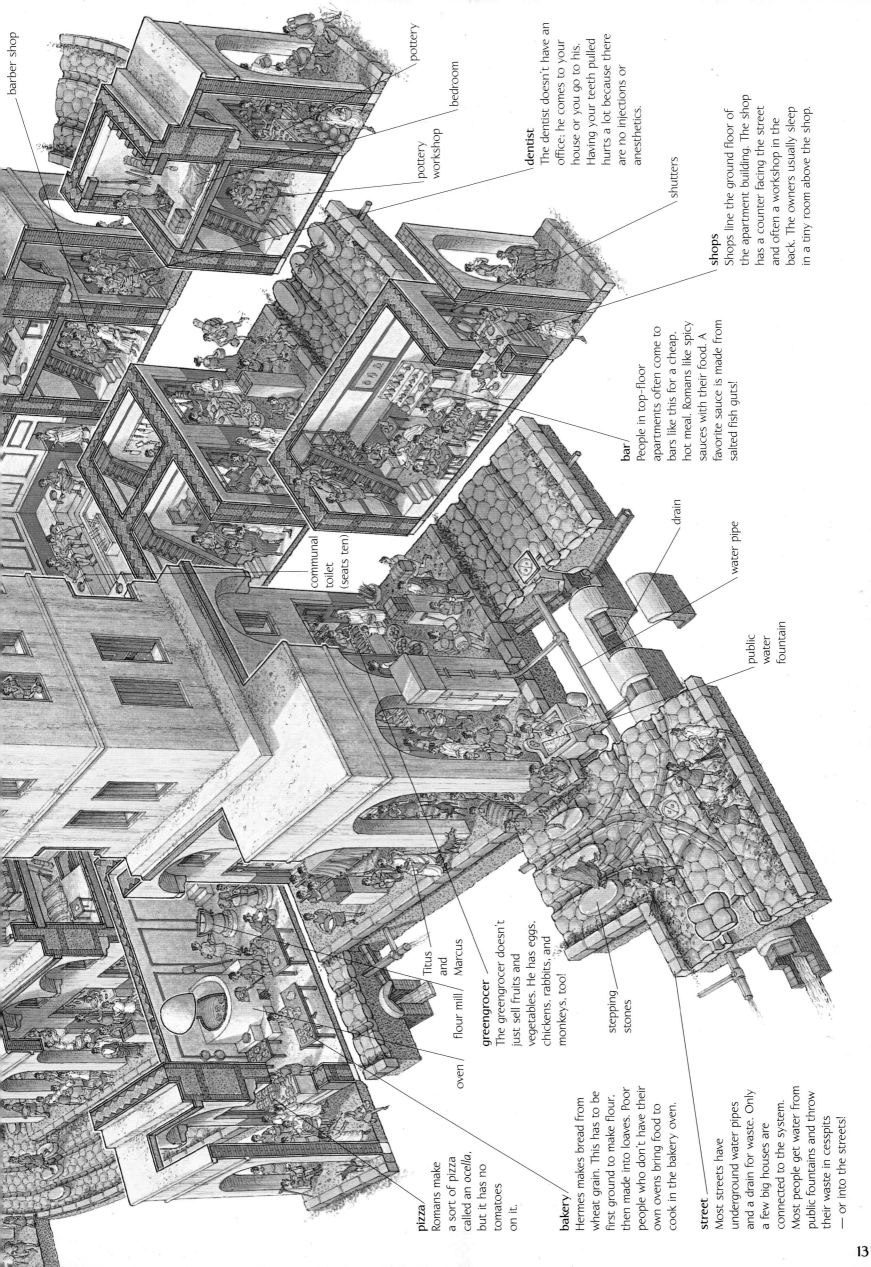

barber shop

pottery

bedroom

pottery workshop

dentist
The dentist doesn't have an office: he comes to your house or you go to his. Having your teeth pulled hurts a lot because there are no injections or anesthetics.

shutters

shops
Shops line the ground floor of the apartment building. The shop has a counter facing the street and often a workshop in the back. The owners usually sleep in a tiny room above the shop.

bar
People in top-floor apartments often come to bars like this for a cheap, hot meal. Romans like spicy sauces with their food. A favorite sauce is made from salted fish guts!

drain

water pipe

communal toilet (seats ten)

public water fountain

Titus and Marcus

greengrocer
The greengrocer doesn't just sell fruits and vegetables. He has eggs, chickens, rabbits, and monkeys, too!

flour mill

stepping stones

oven

pizza
Romans make a sort of pizza called an *ocella*, but it has no tomatoes on it.

bakery
Hermes makes bread from wheat grain. This has to be first ground to make flour, then made into loaves. Poor people who don't have their own ovens bring food to cook in the bakery oven.

street
Most streets have underground water pipes and a drain for waste. Only a few big houses are connected to the system. Most people get water from public fountains and throw their waste in cesspits — or into the streets!

13

The Temple of Jupiter

There are lots of festival days each year, but Titus likes the festival of Castor and Pollux. Castor and Pollux are gods of horsemen, and so the parade includes hundreds of Roman cavalrymen. Titus loves watching the cavalrymen on their fine horses. They are wearing their best armor, and their shining bronze helmets and breastplates gleam in the sun. Titus and his father watch the horsemen pass, then join the parade.

Temple

The Temple itself is very beautiful. The columns are milky white marble, while the roof and doors are covered in gold. Inside there are huge gold and ivory statues of three gods: Jupiter, Juno, and Minerva.

The ceremony

At the start of the ceremony, the priest tosses incense into the altar flame and sprinkles wine and cakes on the altar. Next he offers up a prayer to Castor and Pollux. Now the animals are sacrificed. An official stuns each animal with a hammer, then another official kills it. Some of the meat from the sacrifices is burned on the altar fires. Afterward, the worshippers feast on the meat that is not burned.

During the 3rd hour (8:10 A.M.)

The legend of Castor and Pollux

Hundreds of years ago, the Romans fought a battle against a group of enemies at Lake Regillus, southeast of Rome. The fight was going badly for the Romans until two shining young men named Castor and Pollux appeared on white horses and led them to victory. Later that day, the same men were seen watering their tired horses at a fountain in the Forum. They told the citizens about the victory at Lake Regillus and then disappeared. The temple of Castor and Pollux was built on the site of the fountain in the Forum.

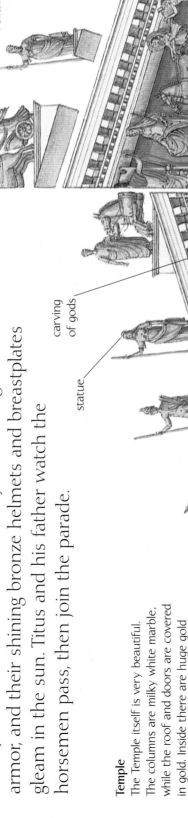

statue

gold covering on tiles

bronze roof tiles

capital (top) of column

carving of gods

statue

Minerva statue

Jupiter statue

Juno statue

marble columns made of smaller drums

golden doors

marble drum

14

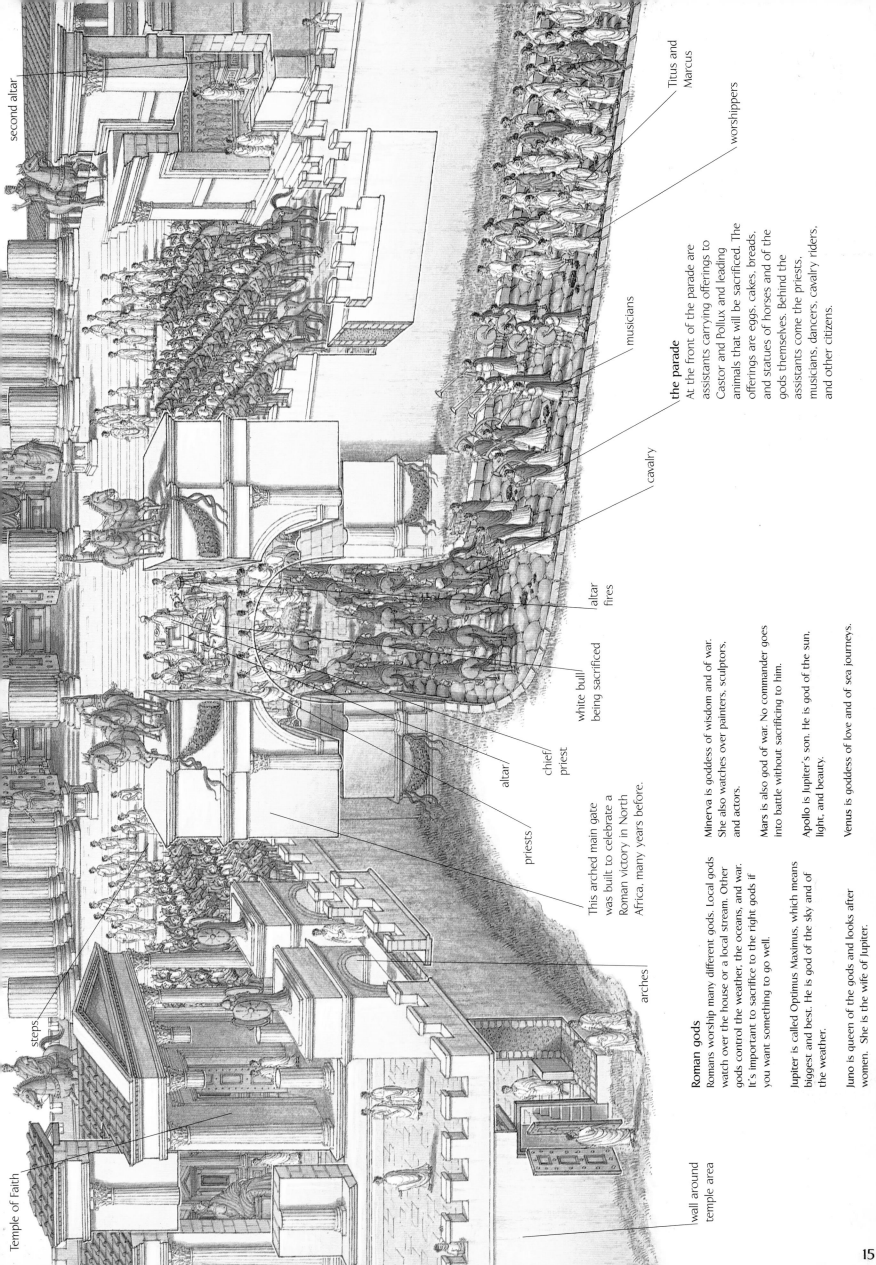

second altar

Titus and Marcus

worshippers

musicians

the parade
At the front of the parade are assistants carrying offerings to Castor and Pollux and leading animals that will be sacrificed. The offerings are eggs, cakes, breads, and statues of horses and of the gods themselves. Behind the assistants come the priests, musicians, dancers, cavalry riders, and other citizens.

cavalry

altar fires

white bull being sacrificed

chief priest

altar

priests

This arched main gate was built to celebrate a Roman victory in North Africa, many years before.

Roman gods
Romans worship many different gods. Local gods watch over the house or a local stream. Other gods control the weather, the oceans, and war. It's important to sacrifice to the right gods if you want something to go well.

Jupiter is called Optimus Maximus, which means biggest and best. He is god of the sky and of the weather.

Juno is queen of the gods and looks after women. She is the wife of Jupiter.

Minerva is goddess of wisdom and of war. She also watches over painters, sculptors, and actors.

Mars is also god of war. No commander goes into battle without sacrificing to him.

Apollo is Jupiter's son. He is god of the sun, light, and beauty.

Venus is goddess of love and of sea journeys.

arches

wall around temple area

steps

Temple of Faith

15

The Forum Romanum

After the parade, Titus and his father head for the games at the Colosseum. On their way through the Forum Romanum, they meet another senator, named Antony. Marcus and Antony run a business together, bringing olive oil from Spain to Rome. Antony says that a ship has just arrived with a new cargo of olive oil. "I'll go to the docks later to check the cargo," says Marcus.

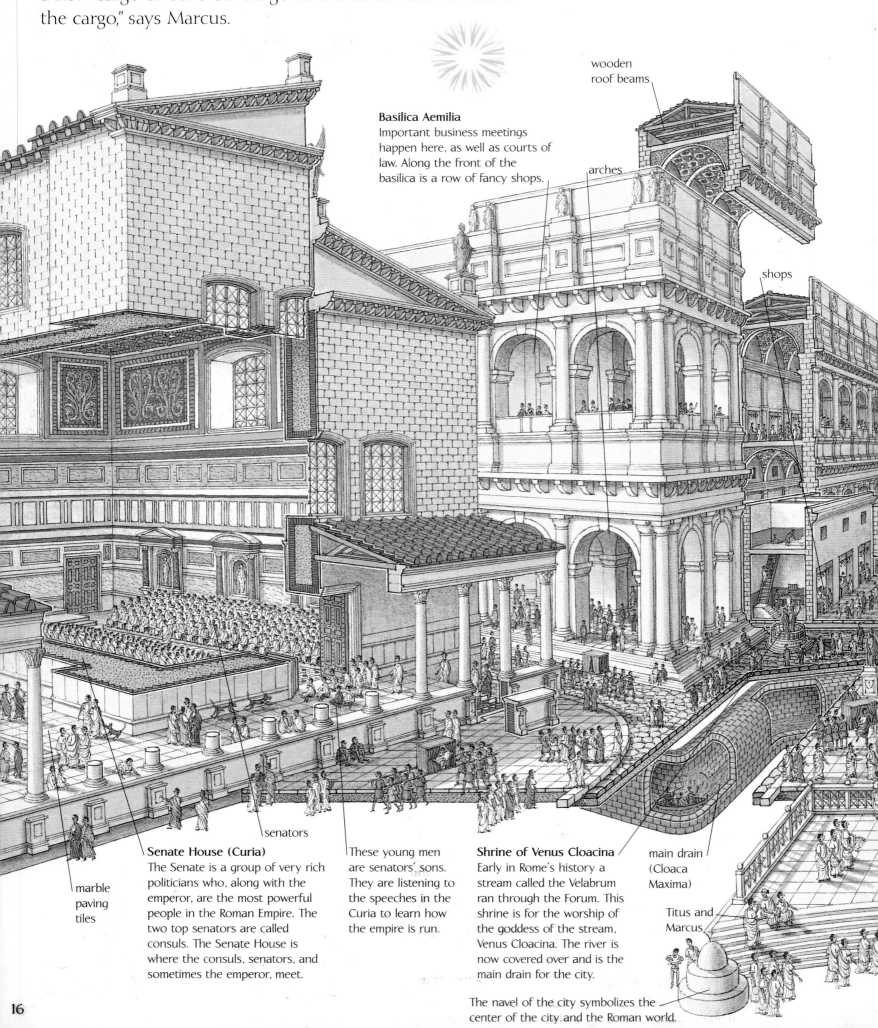

Basilica Aemilia
Important business meetings happen here, as well as courts of law. Along the front of the basilica is a row of fancy shops.

wooden roof beams

arches

shops

senators

marble paving tiles

Senate House (Curia)
The Senate is a group of very rich politicians who, along with the emperor, are the most powerful people in the Roman Empire. The two top senators are called consuls. The Senate House is where the consuls, senators, and sometimes the emperor, meet.

These young men are senators' sons. They are listening to the speeches in the Curia to learn how the empire is run.

Shrine of Venus Cloacina
Early in Rome's history a stream called the Velabrum ran through the Forum. This shrine is for the worship of the goddess of the stream, Venus Cloacina. The river is now covered over and is the main drain for the city.

main drain (Cloaca Maxima)

Titus and Marcus

The navel of the city symbolizes the center of the city and the Roman world.

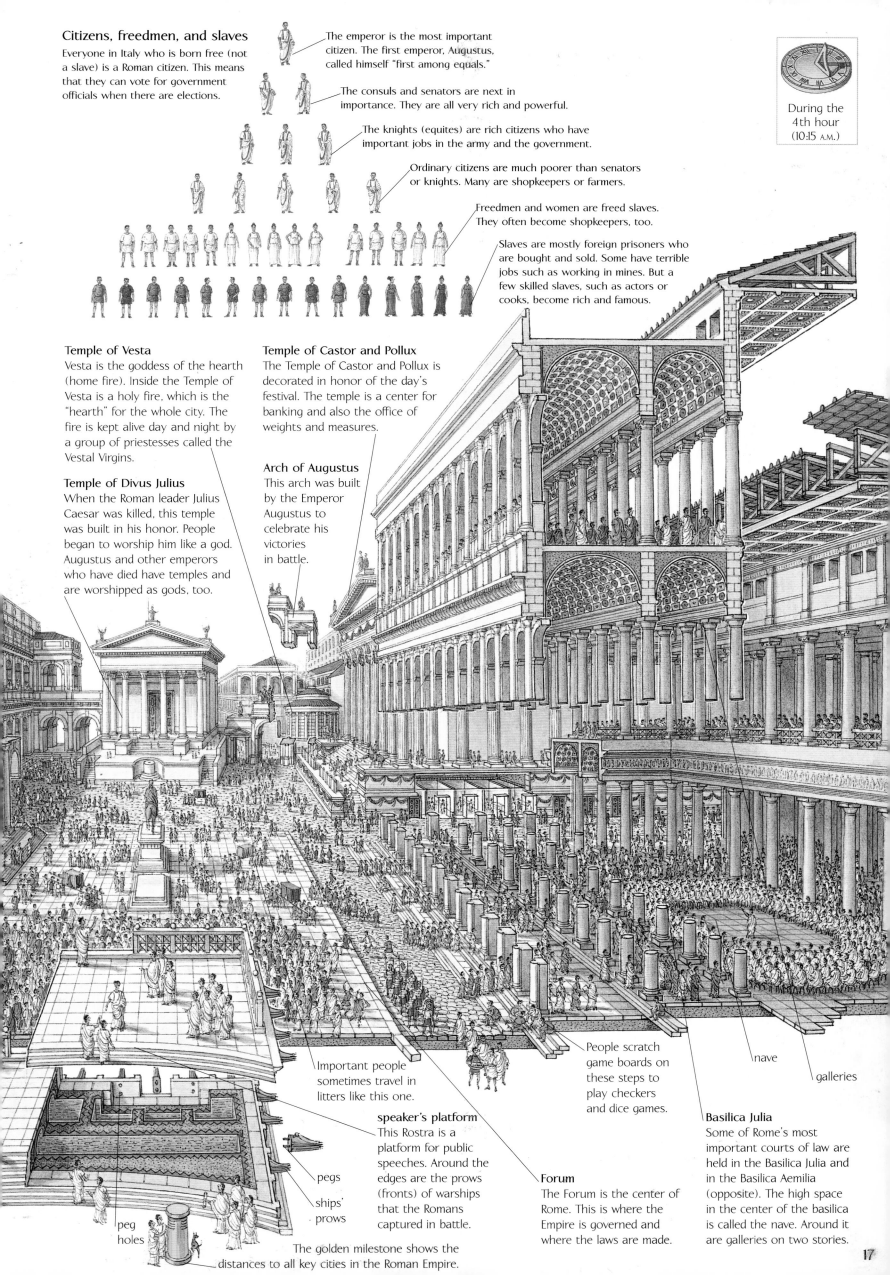

Citizens, freedmen, and slaves
Everyone in Italy who is born free (not a slave) is a Roman citizen. This means that they can vote for government officials when there are elections.

The emperor is the most important citizen. The first emperor, Augustus, called himself "first among equals."

The consuls and senators are next in importance. They are all very rich and powerful.

The knights (equites) are rich citizens who have important jobs in the army and the government.

Ordinary citizens are much poorer than senators or knights. Many are shopkeepers or farmers.

Freedmen and women are freed slaves. They often become shopkeepers, too.

Slaves are mostly foreign prisoners who are bought and sold. Some have terrible jobs such as working in mines. But a few skilled slaves, such as actors or cooks, become rich and famous.

During the 4th hour (10:15 A.M.)

Temple of Vesta
Vesta is the goddess of the hearth (home fire). Inside the Temple of Vesta is a holy fire, which is the "hearth" for the whole city. The fire is kept alive day and night by a group of priestesses called the Vestal Virgins.

Temple of Divus Julius
When the Roman leader Julius Caesar was killed, this temple was built in his honor. People began to worship him like a god. Augustus and other emperors who have died have temples and are worshipped as gods, too.

Temple of Castor and Pollux
The Temple of Castor and Pollux is decorated in honor of the day's festival. The temple is a center for banking and also the office of weights and measures.

Arch of Augustus
This arch was built by the Emperor Augustus to celebrate his victories in battle.

People scratch game boards on these steps to play checkers and dice games.

nave

galleries

Important people sometimes travel in litters like this one.

speaker's platform
This Rostra is a platform for public speeches. Around the edges are the prows (fronts) of warships that the Romans captured in battle.

Forum
The Forum is the center of Rome. This is where the Empire is governed and where the laws are made.

Basilica Julia
Some of Rome's most important courts of law are held in the Basilica Julia and in the Basilica Aemilia (opposite). The high space in the center of the basilica is called the nave. Around it are galleries on two stories.

pegs

ships' prows

peg holes

The golden milestone shows the distances to all key cities in the Roman Empire.

The Colosseum

Titus is really looking forward to the games; he hasn't been to the Colosseum before. It's early, but the amphitheater is already filled with a roaring crowd of thousands of people. The show starts with some amazing performing elephants. One draws letters in the sand with its foot. Next, the hunters enter, each carrying only a spear. Snarling lions and leopards appear from nowhere and surround the hunters. The big cats attack.

vomitoria
There are 64 entrances (*vomitoria*) to the seating area. This means that if there is a fire or an emergency, everyone can get out quickly.

concrete and brick
The upper parts of the building are made of brick and concrete. Roman concrete is waterproof and strengthens with age.

Colossus
The Colossus gives the Colosseum its name. It is a statue of the sun god, Helios, and is about 100 feet tall.

stone posts to anchor the awning ropes to the masts

construction
Seven rings of pillars hold up the Colosseum, with 80 pillars in each ring. More than half a million tons of stone were used in the lower levels of the building.

entrances
There are 76 public entrances to the Colosseum. It is free to enter, but you must have a numbered ticket. The number tells you which entrance you must use.

sand

animal cages
Wild animals are held in these cages before they go into the arena.

Gladiators
Gladiators are criminals, slaves, or prisoners captured in war. Pairs of gladiators are forced to fight to the death. The *hoplomachus* and the *secutor* are heavily armed gladiators. They each have a helmet, a large shield, and a straight sword. The Thracian and the *retiarius* are more lightly armed. Lightest armed of all are the *venatores*, or wild-animal hunters. They have no shields and are armed only with spears.

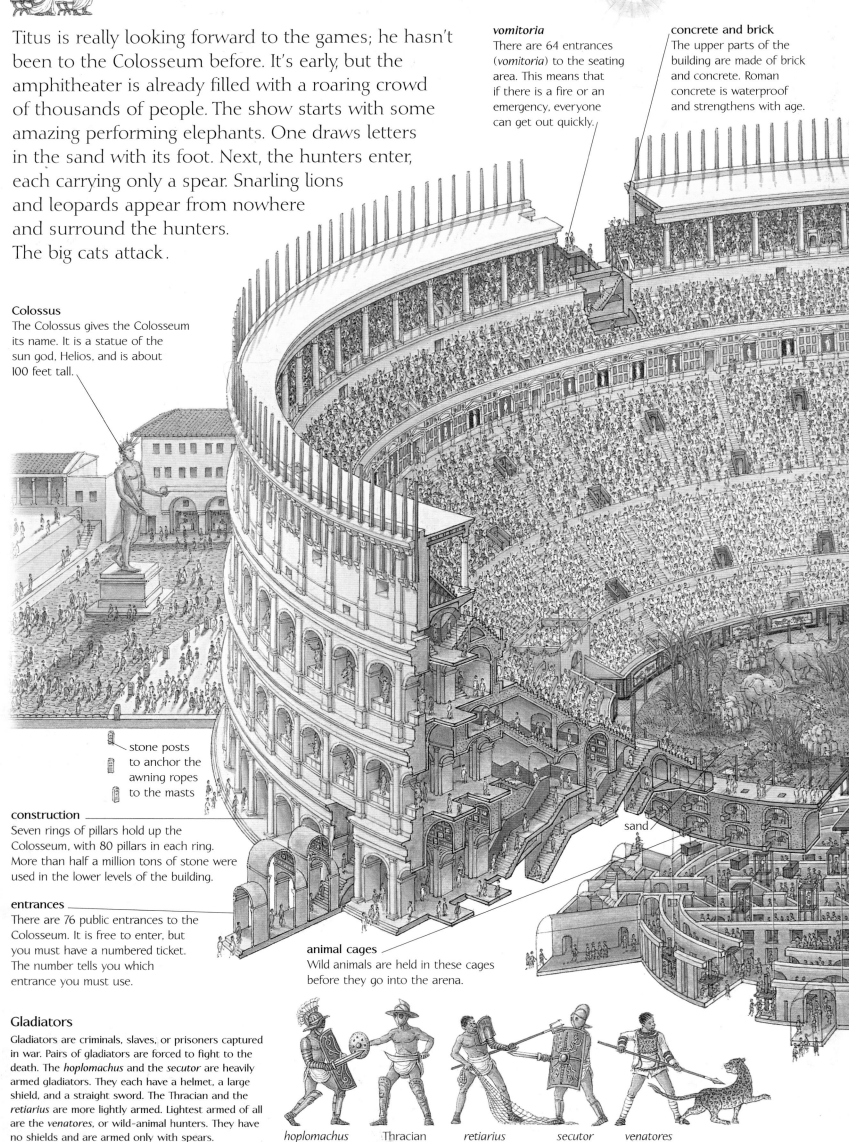

hoplomachus   Thracian   *retiarius*   *secutor*   *venatores*

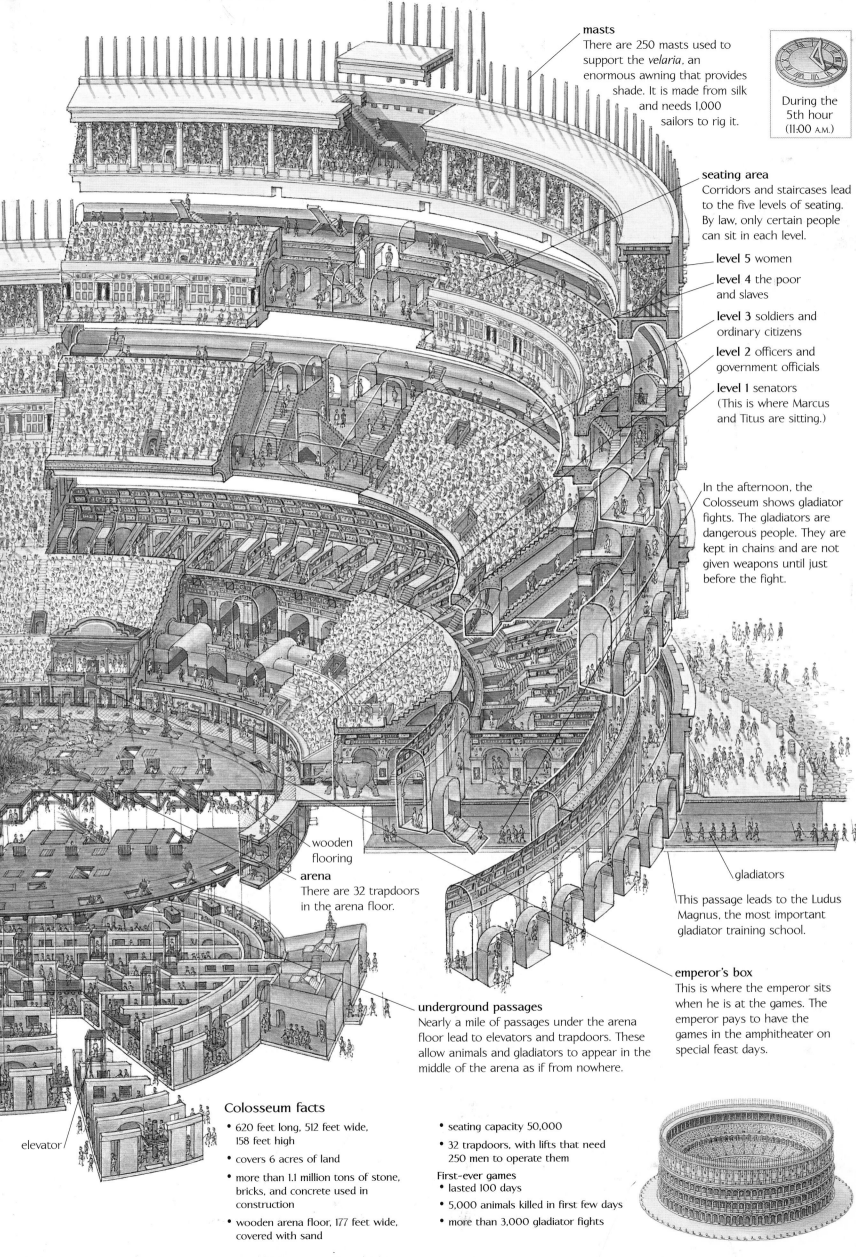

masts
There are 250 masts used to support the *velaria*, an enormous awning that provides shade. It is made from silk and needs 1,000 sailors to rig it.

During the 5th hour (11:00 A.M.)

seating area
Corridors and staircases lead to the five levels of seating. By law, only certain people can sit in each level.

level 5 women

level 4 the poor and slaves

level 3 soldiers and ordinary citizens

level 2 officers and government officials

level 1 senators
(This is where Marcus and Titus are sitting.)

In the afternoon, the Colosseum shows gladiator fights. The gladiators are dangerous people. They are kept in chains and are not given weapons until just before the fight.

wooden flooring

arena
There are 32 trapdoors in the arena floor.

gladiators
This passage leads to the Ludus Magnus, the most important gladiator training school.

emperor's box
This is where the emperor sits when he is at the games. The emperor pays to have the games in the amphitheater on special feast days.

underground passages
Nearly a mile of passages under the arena floor lead to elevators and trapdoors. These allow animals and gladiators to appear in the middle of the arena as if from nowhere.

elevator

Colosseum facts
- 620 feet long, 512 feet wide, 158 feet high
- covers 6 acres of land
- more than 1.1 million tons of stone, bricks, and concrete used in construction
- wooden arena floor, 177 feet wide, covered with sand
- seating capacity 50,000
- 32 trapdoors, with lifts that need 250 men to operate them

First-ever games
- lasted 100 days
- 5,000 animals killed in first few days
- more than 3,000 gladiator fights

At the docks

Titus's father has to go to the docks to check on his cargo of olive oil. Everyone at the docks is incredibly busy. Crane ropes creak, oxen bellow, and the air smells of wine, olives, and sweaty bodies. Grumpy porters yell and jostle anyone who gets in their way. *Oof!* One of them bashes into Titus.

Titus's father talks to an official about his cargo. They go to make sure that the oil is good quality.

Goods from around the world

A city of more than a million people eats a lot! Every day, merchants bring in many tons of food and other goods from all over the known world. There is wheat, building stone, and papyrus from Egypt; wine from Greece and Gaul (France); wool, pottery, and perfumes from Syria and Arabia; wood and horses from Dacia (Eastern Europe); wild animals from North Africa; gold, copper, oil, and wine from Spain; and wool, tin, and iron from Britannia (Britain).

Large ships bringing food and other cargo cannot get up the Tiber River, so they unload at the port of Ostia on the coast. The ship's cargo is then loaded onto barges and pulled up the river by teams of oxen.

Monte Testaccio ("hill of pots")

This hill is about 100 feet high, taller than four houses, and it's made entirely of broken pots! Used olive oil amphoras are dumped here because they become smelly and can't be used again. Walls divide each level of the hill into small areas to stop the whole thing from collapsing. The pots are covered with lime to keep them from smelling.

towpath

team of oxen

empty barges returning to Ostia

Tiber River

← To Ostia

shelving for amphoras

vaulted (arched) ceiling

sacks of grain

wool

donkeys carrying amphoras

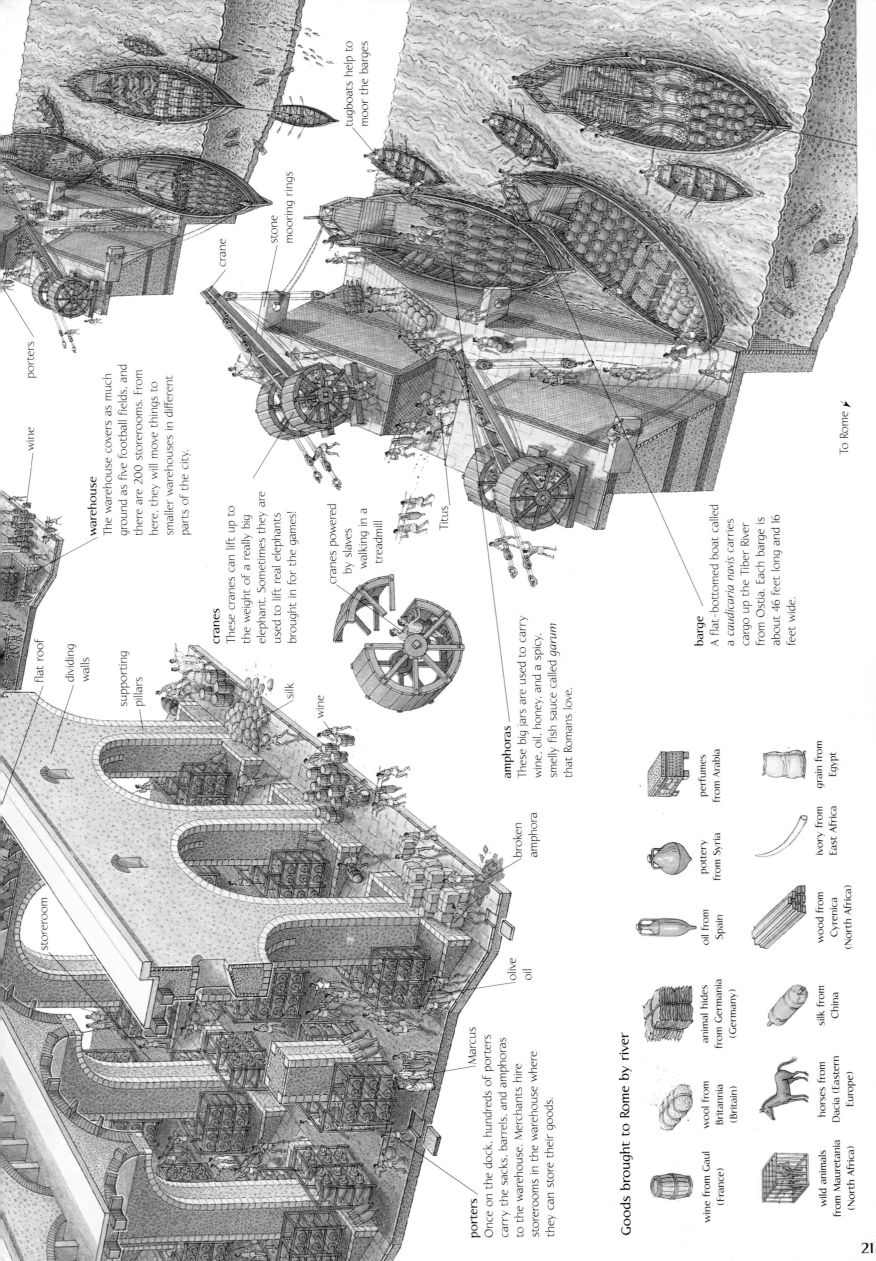

tugboats help to moor the barges

stone mooring rings

crane

warehouse
The warehouse covers as much ground as five football fields, and there are 200 storerooms. From here, they will move things to smaller warehouses in different parts of the city.

porters

wine

cranes
These cranes can lift up to the weight of a really big elephant. Sometimes they are used to lift real elephants brought in for the games!

cranes powered by slaves walking in a treadmill

Titus

amphoras
These big jars are used to carry wine, oil, honey, and a spicy, smelly fish sauce called *garum* that Romans love.

barge
A flat-bottomed boat called a *caudicaria navis* carries cargo up the Tiber River from Ostia. Each barge is about 46 feet long and 16 feet wide.

To Rome ↙

silk

wine

flat roof

dividing walls

supporting pillars

storeroom

broken amphora

olive oil

Marcus

porters
Once on the dock, hundreds of porters carry the sacks, barrels, and amphoras to the warehouse. Merchants hire storerooms in the warehouse where they can store their goods.

Goods brought to Rome by river

perfumes from Arabia

grain from Egypt

pottery from Syria

ivory from East Africa

oil from Spain

wood from Cyrenica (North Africa)

wool from Britannia (Britain)

animal hides from Germania (Germany)

silk from China

wine from Gaul (France)

horses from Dacia (Eastern Europe)

wild animals from Mauretania (North Africa)

The Baths of Trajan

After the dock visit, Titus and his father go to relax and wash at the baths. They meet lots of friends there. Titus swims while his father plays ball and has a massage. Then they soak in the hot tub before taking a refreshing plunge in the cold pool. Titus's father buys them both a drink before they leave.

All Romans enjoy coming to the baths. It is not just a place to wash. People exercise, have a massage, talk business, have a bite to eat, go for a walk, read, or just relax and chat with friends. Women and men usually bathe at different times, women in the morning and men in the mid-afternoon.

ceiling
The vaulted (arched) ceiling is made of concrete. The square decorations are called coffers, and they help give the ceiling strength.

Changing rooms
In the changing rooms (not shown here), there are open lockers where you can leave your clothes. People pay a slave to look after their belongings.

swimming pool
Swimming is a popular way to exercise. Before the public baths were built, many Romans kept fit by swimming across the Tiber River every day.

drains
Drains collect water from all parts of the baths. The drains eventually flow to the Tiber River.

food and drink sellers

cold pool

cold room (*frigidarium*)
Bathers usually finish off with a refreshing plunge in a cold pool in the *frigidarium*.

hot tubs

Scraping themselves clean
Romans don't wash with soap. First, they exercise or sunbathe to get themselves sweaty. Then they get a slave attendant to rub their skin with oil. Finally, the slave scrapes off the oil and dirt using a scraper called a strigil.

warm room (*tepidarium*)
The *tepidarium* is warm; it's a place to cool off a little after the *caldarium*.

hot room (*caldarium*)
People start by relaxing in steaming hot water tubs in the hot room (*caldarium*).

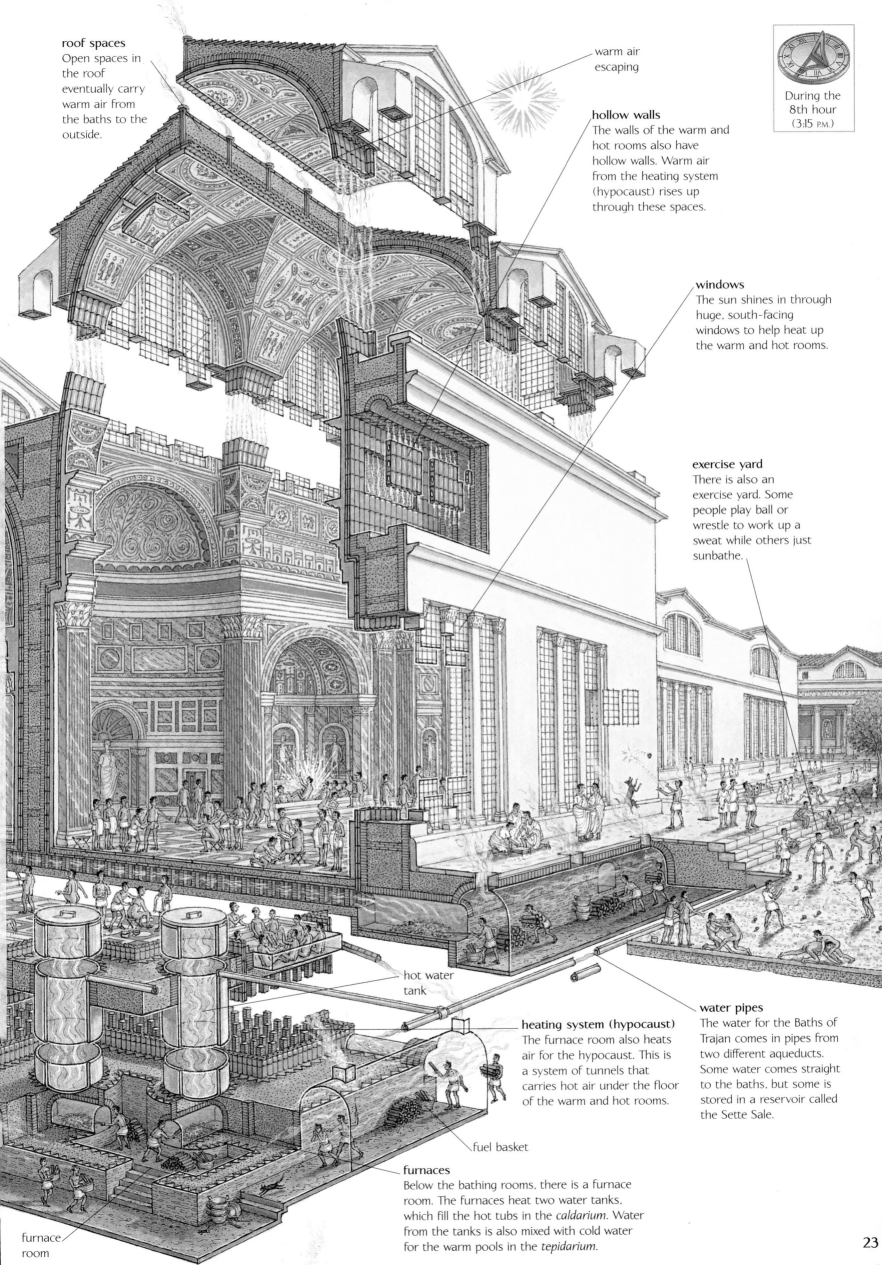

roof spaces
Open spaces in the roof eventually carry warm air from the baths to the outside.

warm air escaping

hollow walls
The walls of the warm and hot rooms also have hollow walls. Warm air from the heating system (hypocaust) rises up through these spaces.

windows
The sun shines in through huge, south-facing windows to help heat up the warm and hot rooms.

exercise yard
There is also an exercise yard. Some people play ball or wrestle to work up a sweat while others just sunbathe.

During the 8th hour (3:15 P.M.)

hot water tank

water pipes
The water for the Baths of Trajan comes in pipes from two different aqueducts. Some water comes straight to the baths, but some is stored in a reservoir called the Sette Sale.

heating system (hypocaust)
The furnace room also heats air for the hypocaust. This is a system of tunnels that carries hot air under the floor of the warm and hot rooms.

fuel basket

furnaces
Below the bathing rooms, there is a furnace room. The furnaces heat two water tanks, which fill the hot tubs in the *caldarium*. Water from the tanks is also mixed with cold water for the warm pools in the *tepidarium*.

furnace room

23

At the races

The best treat of the day is the chariot races at the Circus Maximus. Everyone is shouting for their favorite team. Titus and his father support the Green team. "Come on Greens!" Titus yells. But on the first turn, a Red charioteer swings around too tightly and his chariot turns over — right in the path of one of the Green chariots. Luckily, the drivers are unhurt. They struggle to cut their horses free before the other chariots come around again.

Circus Maximus
The Circus Maximus is the biggest stadium ever! It is nearly 2,000 feet long — bigger than any modern sports stadium. It holds 250,000 people. The Circus was first laid out by Rome's King Tarquin, in about 500 B.C.

spina
The *spina* runs down the middle of the circus like the guardrail on a highway. Three pillars at either end mark the turning points.

starting gates
The starting gates have separate boxes for each chariot. A trumpet sounds to start the race. A clever mechanism makes all twelve gates spring open at once, and the chariots charge out.

starting boxes

spring-operated starting gates

dolphin statues

water pools
Each team has a water pool on the *spina*. As their chariots go past, slaves throw water on the sweating horses.

snack seller

betting
All through the crowd, people are betting on who will win the race. Roman law says that betting is illegal, but no one seems to mind!

Titus and Marcus

chariot teams
Each chariot and charioteer belongs to one of four teams: Reds, Whites, Greens, or Blues. There are twelve chariots in the race, three from each team. These chariots are *quadrigas* (four-horse teams).

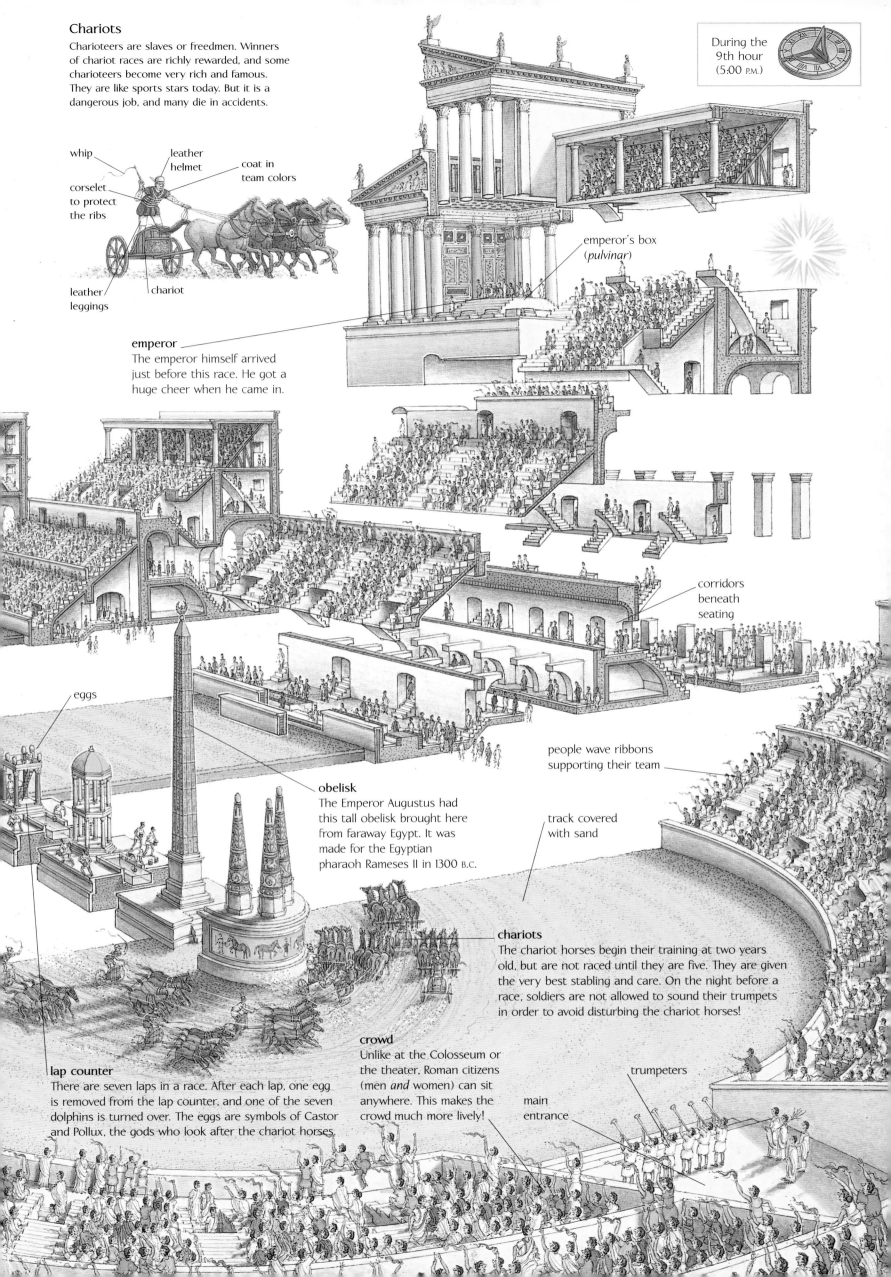

Chariots

Charioteers are slaves or freedmen. Winners of chariot races are richly rewarded, and some charioteers become very rich and famous. They are like sports stars today. But it is a dangerous job, and many die in accidents.

whip

leather helmet

coat in team colors

corselet to protect the ribs

leather leggings

chariot

emperor's box (*pulvinar*)

emperor
The emperor himself arrived just before this race. He got a huge cheer when he came in.

corridors beneath seating

eggs

obelisk
The Emperor Augustus had this tall obelisk brought here from faraway Egypt. It was made for the Egyptian pharaoh Rameses II in 1300 B.C.

people wave ribbons supporting their team

track covered with sand

chariots
The chariot horses begin their training at two years old, but are not raced until they are five. They are given the very best stabling and care. On the night before a race, soldiers are not allowed to sound their trumpets in order to avoid disturbing the chariot horses!

crowd
Unlike at the Colosseum or the theater, Roman citizens (men *and* women) can sit anywhere. This makes the crowd much more lively!

lap counter
There are seven laps in a race. After each lap, one egg is removed from the lap counter, and one of the seven dolphins is turned over. The eggs are symbols of Castor and Pollux, the gods who look after the chariot horses.

trumpeters

main entrance

Home again

When Titus and his father get back from the chariot races, it's time for supper. Titus eats in the kitchen. He is too young to go to the grown-ups' feast.

Before Titus goes to bed, his father comes in with a package. "I got this for you at the Colosseum," he says. "It's a model gladiator!"

Food

On normal days, the family eats simple food, such as bread, cheese, vegetables, olives, and a little meat. At a dinner party, the food is rich and spicy. Romans like spicy sauces with their food. A favorite one is *garum*, or *liquamen*, which is made from fish that have been left to rot in the sun for several days!

doorkeeper
The doorkeeper bars the house door and brings the guard dog from its kennel.

guard dog

street
At night the streets are noisy and dangerous. There are no street lights, so it's very dark. Huge carts constantly rumble up and down the streets, and there are thieves waiting to pounce on people.

shops
The bronzesmith is closing up his shop for the night. He covers the front with large shutters.

night watchmen
A band of night watchmen patrol the streets. They try to stop robbers and other criminals, but there aren't really enough of them to make the streets safe.

torchbearer

Titus's bedroom
Titus lies in bed with his model gladiator, and listens to the music and laughter from the dining room. He is beginning to feel very sleepy.

chamber pot

litter

Fulvia's room
Baby Fulvia is already asleep. The nanny dozes in a chair by the cradle.

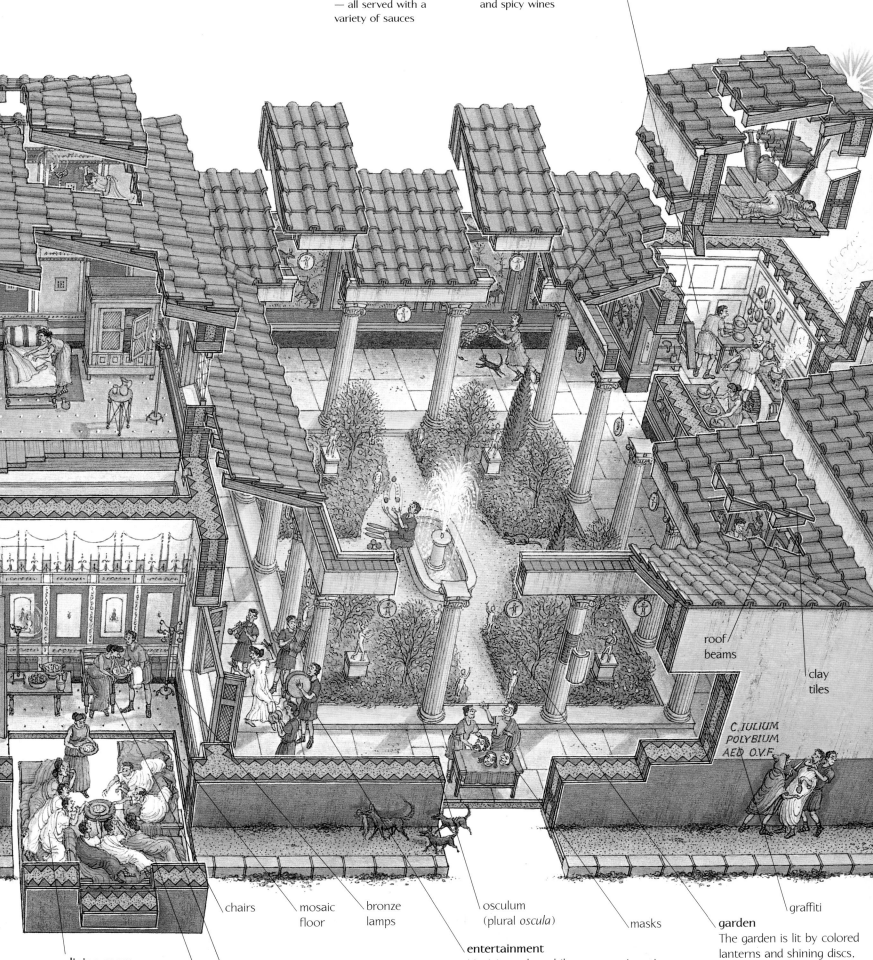

MENU

gustatio (appetizers)
- eggs
- salads
- radishes
- mushrooms
- olives
- oysters
- bread rolls

prima mensa (main meal)
- a roasted pig
- boiled pig's udders
- fried chicken with leeks
- boiled veal (calf)
- pigeons
- snails fattened on milk
- sea mussels
- tuna
— all served with a variety of sauces

secunda mensa (dessert)
- pear soufflé
- pancakes with milk
- pastries
- fresh fruit
- nuts

To drink
- a selection of sweet and spicy wines

kitchen
The slaves in the kitchen are busy setting out food on dishes. Chilo is already grumpy because his best helper is ill in bed. Now his replacement has just dropped a whole tray of pastries!

During the 11th hour (8:00 P.M.)

roof beams

clay tiles

C. IULIUM POLYBIUM AED O.V.F.

graffiti

garden
The garden is lit by colored lanterns and shining discs, called *oscula*, flash in the lamplight. The actor practices with his masks while he waits to entertain the guests.

chairs

mosaic floor

bronze lamps

osculum (plural *oscula*)

masks

dining room
In the dining room, Titus's parents have guests for dinner. The men and women eat lying on couches or sitting on chairs.

wooden couches

cloths and cushions

entertainment
Musicians play while everyone is eating. Later, a famous actor will dance and perform a funny play for the guests. There is sweet and spicy wine with the meal, but after dessert, the men will drink more wine and talk until late in the night.

Glossary

altar: a flat-topped stone block where priests sacrificed animals to the gods.

amphitheater: a round, open building with tiers of seats, where gladiator contests and wild animal hunts took place.

amphora: a large, round-bottomed pottery jar, used for storing such things as olive oil, wine, and fish sauce.

Apollo: the Roman god of light, music, and poetry.

aqueduct: an artificial channel for carrying water. Rome had 10 aqueducts, bringing water from rivers as far as 40 miles away.

atrium: a large hallway at the front of a Roman house. The roof of the atrium was open at the center, and there was a pool to catch rainwater under the opening.

Augustus: the first Roman emperor. He ruled the empire for 41 years, from 27 B.C. to A.D. 14. Before Augustus, the empire was run by the Senate and the consuls.

basilica: a large building with an open space in the center and colonnades (walkways lined with columns) along the sides. Basilicas were used for courts of law and as places for holding large meetings.

caldarium: the hot room of the Roman baths.

Castor and Pollux: twin Roman gods, the gods of horsemen, sailors, and of friendship. Castor was a horse tamer, Pollux a boxer.

cesspit: a deep hole used for garbage and sewage.

Circus Maximus: the largest chariot-racing arena in Rome. All chariot racetracks were called circuses, and maximus means "biggest."

clients: poorer citizens who relied on someone rich and powerful (their patron) for work and protection. In return, the clients helped the patron and did jobs for him, especially at election times.

Colosseum: the largest amphitheater in Rome, where emperors held gladiator games.

consuls: the two top Roman officials. In the time of the emperors, one of the consuls was often the emperor. The consuls were elected every year.

corselet: a close-fitting, sleeveless leather jacket worn to protect the body.

Curia: the building at the center of Rome where the emperor and the senators (Rome's richest and most powerful people) met to discuss the running of the empire.

Domitian: emperor of Rome from A.D. 81 to 96.

elections: events where people voted to choose who would be the consuls, judges, and other officials in charge of running the empire.

equites: Romans who were wealthy but not as well-off as senators. Many of them were involved in running the empire or had important jobs in the army.

forum: a public square or marketplace. There were many forums in Rome and in the many towns and cities of the empire. The most important one was the Forum Romanum (Roman Forum) in the center of Rome.

freedman or **freedwoman:** a man or woman who had been a slave but who was now free. Slaves were freed by their masters if they served them well for a long time. Slaves could also buy their freedom, if they could earn enough money to do so.

frigidarium: the cold room of the Roman baths.

garum: see *liquamen.*

gladiator: someone who fought in the amphitheater to entertain people. Most gladiators were prisoners of war or criminals. They were forced to fight, often to the death. However, a successful gladiator could become rich and famous.

Hadrian: emperor of Rome from A.D. 117 to 138, including the time of our story.

Helios: the Roman sun god. The giant Colossus statue, which gave the Colosseum its name, was a statue of Helios.

hoplomachus: the most common heavily armed gladiator. The *hoplomachus* carried a large rectangular shield and a straight sword.

hypocaust: underfloor central heating. This type of heating was widely used in Roman public buildings and larger houses.

impluvium: the pool below the opening in the atrium roof, where rainwater collected.

incense: a substance that gives off a sweet or spicy smell when it is burned. Incense was burned in Roman temples, especially during religious ceremonies.

Juno: the chief Roman goddess, wife of Jupiter.

Jupiter: the most important Roman god, god of the sky and weather.

lararium: the shrine (worshipping place) of the Roman household gods.

liquamen (garum): a very spicy fish sauce, widely used by Romans in their cooking.

Ludus Magnus: the largest training school for gladiators in Rome. A tunnel connected it to the Colosseum.

Mars: the Roman god of war.

Minerva: the Roman goddess of wisdom, and also of war.

mosaic: a covering for a floor or wall, made from many colored pieces of glass or stone fitted together to make a picture or pattern.

nave: the central part of a Roman basilica. The name later came to be used for the central part of a church.

obelisk: a tapering, usually four-sided, stone pillar.

ocella: a Roman snack, consisting of a flat round of bread topped with olives and cheese. It was similar to a modern pizza, but had no tomatoes (tomatoes were not grown in Europe in Roman times).

osculum: a disc made of metal or other shiny substances that was hung up in such a way as to flash when it caught the light.

Ostia: the main port for Rome. Rome is on the Tiber River, but large boats could not sail up the river because it was too shallow. They had to unload at the coast, at Ostia.

papyrus: a paperlike material made from reeds. Papyrus was first made in ancient Egypt.

pharaoh: the Egyptian king in ancient times.

portico: a flat roof, supported by pillars, that forms a porch to a building. Porticoes were built on apartment buildings in Rome to help firefighters reach the upper floors in a fire.

Praetorian Guard: the soldiers of the emperor's personal bodyguard.

quadriga: a four-horse chariot.

retiarius: a lightly armed gladiator. A *retiarius* had no shield, but carried a trident and a net.

Rostra: a platform in the Roman Forum where important speeches were made.

sacrifice: an animal that was sacrificed (killed) as part of a religious ceremony.

secutor: a type of Roman gladiator. The *secutor* was heavily armed, with a helmet, sword, and shield. His helmet was smooth, to avoid getting caught in the net of a *retiarius.*

Senate House: the meeting place for the Senate, the group of rich, powerful politicians who, along with the emperor, ran the empire.

senator: a member of the Senate.

Sette Sale: a reservoir where water for the Baths of Trajan was stored.

spina: the "center strip" running down the middle of the Circus Maximus.

strigil: a scraper, used to scrape oil from the skin. Romans did not wash with soap, instead, they oiled themselves and then scraped off the dirty oil to get clean.

Tarquin: in the earliest times Rome was ruled by kings. Tarquin was the fourth of Rome's seven kings. He ruled from 616 to 579 B.C.

tepidarium: the warm room of the Roman baths.

toga: a garment worn by Roman men that consisted of a large piece of woolen cloth draped about the body.

Trajan: emperor of Rome from A.D. 98 to 117.

tunic: a piece of clothing, consisting of a rectangle of cloth with a hole for the head, held by a belt at the waist.

vault: an arched ceiling. Vaulted roofs can span larger distances between supports than a flat roof.

venatores: wild animal hunters, part of the entertainment at the amphitheater.

Venus: Roman goddess of love.

vomitoria: entrances and exits in the Colosseum seating area.

Index